WHEN GOD LEFT A MESSAGE ON MY LAPTOP!

And other amazing testimonies of Divine Intervention in our time

Dr R. Peprah-Gyamfi

Thank You Jesus Books

Published by **Thank You Jesus Books**

www.peprah-gyamfi.com
email: **info@peprah-gyamfi.com**

ISBN: **9781913285036**
eISBN: **9781913285043**

Table of Contents

"In the same hour came forth fingers of a man's hand, and wrote over against the candlestick upon the plaister of the wall of the king's palace: and the king saw the part of the hand that wrote."

Daniel 5:5 (KJV)

Saturday April 25, 2020, 07:20 hrs local time.

I was seated in front of my laptop. I was writing sermons and meditations as well as reflections on various socio-political issues of our day from a Christian perspective.

I had just opened a Microsoft Word document and began writing my thoughts; even before I could save the document, all of a sudden the message *"Wishes can never fill a sack!"* appeared at the top of the screen! Incredible but true. I was witnessing my "writing on the wall" experience—in a twenty-first-century setting!

.

Preface

C hild of God, is the battle going against you? Are you battered from all sides by the enemy—one problem goes, only to be replaced by a more challenging one?

Are you burdened with a host of problems, problems that are threatening to break your neck? In the face of your problems, are you inclined to listen to the insinuations, the lies of the Enemy, the Enemy sowing seeds of doubt in your heart, urging you to doubt the existence of the "I am that I AM"?

Have you been adversely affected by the COVID-19 outbreak? Have you lost a loved one, or loved ones, to this awful ailment? Perhaps one day they were with you and, a few days later, their lifeless bodies were deposited in the morgue!

Has the heart-breaking experience led you to doubt Almighty God, even question His existence? And if He does indeed exist, why does He permit such terrible things to visit your home?

Child of God, has your own personal tragedy, compounded by the unceasing grim news of the world brought into your living room by TV, led you to question the existence of Almighty God, even to begin to question whether there is any God at all? Perhaps you have begun to wonder if you have believed in vain, to question whether the Biblical accounts of His working in the lives of others—Abraham, Moses, Samuel, etc.—were after all fabrications, fake news, fairy tales!

Despairing child of God, I urge you to hold on, hold on! We do indeed serve a living God; indeed, the God we serve has not changed. He is the same yesterday, today and forever.

Why am I so sure? His presence is manifested in His creation. He also sent His son Jesus Christ to demonstrate His power.

Nevertheless, I also felt abandoned recently.

Just as I felt abandoned, the Rock of Ages manifested Himself in a spectacular manner in my life, in a manner that was not only unexpected, but also beyond anything that I could imagine in my wildest dreams. He sent a message straight to me on my laptop!

I am not crazy; indeed, I have not gone bananas! My revelation is not a fabrication—I am not lying. I am telling the truth, nothing but the truth.

So I urge you not to lose heart, child of God who might be experiencing extreme anxiety, sorrow, or pain at this time.

The Lord will surely come your way. I cannot tell exactly when the angels of heaven will make a divine call at your home, but come they surely will.

As you wait for Heaven's messengers to knock on your door, I pray for the needed grace for you to endure your trials, your challenges, indeed your suffering.

Prologue

To the one and only God be the glory

I n this book, I have recounted not only the extraordinary Divine manifestation I experienced on April 25, 2020, but also a series of miracles and favours that I attribute to no one else but the Almighty God of Heaven and Earth, the Big-Hearted one, He who causes his sun to rise on the evil and the good, and sends rain on the righteous as well as the unrighteous (Matthew 5:45).

The testimonies are presented in chronological order—the order in which I experienced them. So the main testimony, the testimony that bears the title of this book, is left to the very end. Those who cannot wait until the end to read it are, of course, free to read it right away. To see the bigger picture of the Divine workings in my life, however, I strongly recommend that after you have read the main testimony, you go back and read the whole, indeed to go through the other amazing testimonies as well.

We do indeed serve a living God. It is my hope that the reader will draw inspiration from the testimonies contained in this book. They are told, not to my glory, but to the glory of the Alpha and Omega, the One and only God of creation.

Part 1

I knew you before you knew me

When Jesus saw Nathanael approaching, he said of him, "Here truly is an Israelite in whom there is no deceit."

"How do you know me?" Nathanael asked.

Jesus answered, "I saw you while you were still under the fig tree before Philip called you."

Then Nathanael declared, "Rabbi, you are the Son of God; you are the king of Israel."

John 1:47–49

The main part of this book is devoted to my experience with the Lord after I had made a conscious decision to follow the Lord.

Now, looking back, I realise that even before I made that decision, the Lord "had long spotted me" while I was still wandering the world, indeed that He was fighting for me even before I made the deliberate decision to follow Him.

Looking back at my life journey, I can identify several instances prior to my conversion when the Divine intervened to rescue me from the claws of the destroyer. I shall share only two examples with the reader.

1

Heaven intervening on behalf of a nonentity

I was born into very humble circumstances in the small village Mpintimpi, situated about 150 kilometres to the northwest of Accra, Ghana's capital.

A makeshift bathroom served as the "labour ward". Mother had to endure the terrible labour pains with no healthcare professional around to administer pain relief. She was not left alone, however. Apart from the traditional midwife attending her, angels of the Living Lord were at hand to provide comfort and protection.

Even before I had time to familiarise myself with the planet I had elected to visit, something happened to threaten to cut short my stay here.

I was barely eight months old when a boil developed on the left side of my neck. Over time, it increased in size, threatening to choke me.

There is a common belief that persists to this day in my culture to the effect that handling boils is not within the remit of conventional medicine! My parents decided, therefore, to resort to traditional medicine.

Nevertheless, this showed no sign of being capable of managing the situation. The boil continued to grow and grow in size. The little child, as I was then, was dying!

Eventually, my parents were directed to a traditional healer at Afosu, a comparatively larger settlement almost four miles to the south of our village.

According to my parents, I could hardly breathe as they arrived at the home of the traditional doctor. On seeing my desperate situation, he immediately left for the woods, returning a short while later with some herbs, which he later pounded into a paste and applied to the boil.

Then came the turning point! All of a sudden, as if an invisible hand had used an invisible instrument to cut it open, the boil literally exploded!

I am convinced it was not the herbal paste applied to the boil that made the difference.

As a doctor, I know it was an abscess (boil) harbouring billions, maybe trillions, of bacteria. While my parents kept me at home and did not seek medical help, the germs could have infiltrated my bloodstream to cause blood poisoning, a situation that would with certainty have cut short my stay on Earth.

Yet the Almighty Father, who knew exactly the number of hairs on my head ("But the very hairs of your head are all numbered"—Matthew 10:30) preserved me, a nonentity that I am, from harm, even before I could be in a position to make a conscious decision to follow Him!

2

Rescued by the greatest physician of all time

For I will restore health unto thee, and I will heal thee of thy wounds, saith the LORD; because they called thee an Outcast, saying, This is Zion, whom no man seeketh after.

Jeremiah 30:17 (KJV)

W hen I was growing up there was no school in our village. Children of school-going age had to walk to the Nyafoman settlement, a comparatively larger settlement, about two miles to the north of my village to attend the primary school there.

When I got to Primary 5, something happened to me to threaten an abrupt end of my educational carrier. All of a sudden, and for no apparent cause, my left ankle joint began to swell up. Initially the accompanying discomfort was bearable, permitting me to continue to walk the distance to attend school. In time, however, the pain increased in intensity. Despite the increasing discomfort, I refused initially to stay out of school. I enjoyed going to school and stayed away only when it was absolutely impossible to do so due to ill health.

A time eventually came though when the excruciating pain left me with no choice but to stop going to school. A two-year interruption in my education followed.

Desperate to find a cure for their son, my parents tried various types of traditional medicine. Eventually they took a loan and took me to hospital. Conventional medicine did not lead to an immediate cure, however. Nevertheless, a little over two years since it all began, the pain subsided to the extent that I was able to resume my education.

Undoubtedly, though I had until then not made a conscious decision to follow the Lord, the Good High Priest was mediating for me before the Throne of Grace.

Part 2

Testimonies along the Christian journey

3

The call that changed my life

Behold, I stand at the door, and knock: if any man hears my voice, and open the door, I will come in to him, and will sup with him, and he with me.

Revelation 3:20 (KJV)

In the previous chapter, I testified to the Lord's favour in helping me resume my education after a two-year forced interruption.

A few years after the resumption of my education, I experienced a significant leap forward on my educational journey—I passed an entry exam that permitted me to move from the village elementary school to attend the Oda Secondary School at our district capital, Akim Oda.

After obtaining my GCE O-levels in July 1976, I moved on to the Mfantsipim Secondary School, one of the leading secondary schools in the country, to do my two-year sixth form. Founded in 1876 by Methodist missionaries, it prided itself on being the first secondary school in the country. Located in Cape Coast, a city about 60 miles to the west of Accra, a good number of prominent personalities in the country had passed through its doors.

It was a big leap indeed for the village boy from Mpintimpi. One could compare the situation to that of the child of a cleaner in the UK making it all the way to Oxford or Cambridge!

One Sunday, towards the end of my second and final year at Mfantsipim, rumours began to circulate that one of the students in the junior classes had gone missing. The news reached me quite early, for the person in question happened to be in my dormitory. Later, further details emerged. He had left the previous day to visit his girlfriend at a girls' boarding school in a nearby town. Contrary to his custom, he had failed to return. Since then, all contact with him had been lost.

The dormitory captain reported the matter to the housemaster. Just before he could take further action, two young police officers came to the school to find out whether anyone there was missing. They went on to say that the authorities at the main hospital in the city had notified them about the unclaimed body of a young victim of a traffic accident that had occurred the previous evening. Eventually the dead boy was identified as the missing student.

Still later, details emerged regarding the circumstances of his death. At the end of his visit to his girlfriend he had waited at a bus station to catch a bus to Cape Coast. Just then, a saloon car passed by. The driver offered him a lift and they had gone only a few miles when the vehicle was involved in a serious accident. Our schoolmate was killed instantly.

Although I knew him only casually, his tragic death at the age of about 15 sent shockwaves through me. The sudden awareness that life could end very abruptly came home to me pretty powerfully and gave me food for thought.

Before the body of our companion was driven to his hometown for burial, a memorial service was held in his honour in the large school chapel. At one stage in the solemn service we were permitted to file past the body to pay our last respects to the dead.

That close confrontation with the departed boy, the lifeless body of our compatriot, who a couple of days before was going about his life like any young person of his age, led me to ask myself—where would I spend eternity should the same fate befall me any time soon?

As might be expected, given that Mfantsipim Boys was founded by Methodist missionaries, worship services follow the Methodist tradition. Among the songs we sang on that solemn occasion was Methodist Hymn 157:

Jesus Calls us! Over the tumult
of our life's wild restless sea,
Day by day His sweet voice
soundeth
Saying: Christian follow me.

As of old, apostles heard it
By the Galilean lake,
Turned from home and toil and
kindren
Leaving all for His dear sake.

Jesus calls us from the worship
Of the vain world's golden store,
From each idol that would keep us,
Saying: Christian love Me more!

In our joys and in our sorrows,
Days of toil and hours of ease,
Still He calls, in cares and pleasures,
That we love Him more than
these.

Jesus calls us! By thy mercies,
Saviour, make us hear Thy call
Give our hearts to Thine obedience.
Serve and Love Thee best of all.

I am not a person easily overtaken by emotion. As we sang that song, however, the words touched my heart to the extent that I could hardly suppress my tears. I began to reflect on the hymn. Though I believed in the existence of God and attended church regularly, I could neither boast of a personal relation nor a full commitment to Christ. The bitter realities of this world had all but made a sceptic of me.

Indeed the issue of universal suffering in the presence of a loving God really troubled me. Whenever something terrible happened around me the question sprang up in my mind: if there were a loving God, why should the world be full of so much evil—war, crime, injustice, confusion here, confusion there, confusion everywhere?

Yet on that day, as we were bidding goodbye to our departed classmate, the call of Jesus the Lord came afresh to me, to follow Him; the call was even more forcefully evident in my heart, which, like that of John Wesley, was strangely warmed.

Even as we sang the song, I dipped my hand into my pocket, removed a pen and placed a big mark on the hymn number: 157. That was the only song in the whole book to be singled out in that way.

Over the next several days the death of my schoolmate occupied my mind. The thought that I could face a similar fate at any time would not leave me in peace. Should something like that happen to me, where would I spend eternity?

Soon life returned to normal. I continued to attend the Sunday evening worship service, as was required of every student, without any conscious commitment to leave this "world's vain golden store" to follow Jesus, as the hymn invited me to do.

The two-year sixth-form course at Mfantsipim ended in June 1978. Shortly before we took the series of examinations aimed at the West African Examination Council GCE A-Level certificate, we completed the university admission forms. I selected medicine as my first choice—at the university in Accra as well as in Kumasi. Only two of the three universities in the country offered medicine.

From Cape Coast, I first travelled to my parents at Mpintimpi. After spending a few days there, I left for Accra. My hope was to find vacation employment that would enable me to earn some money prior to beginning my university education in October that year.

I lived in a suburb of Accra known as Asylum Down. One day I took a stroll through the neighbourhood. As I walked around I bumped into an old acquaintance, Grace, who happened to be the cousin of Kwadwo, my best friend and classmate at Oda Secondary School.

I had met her during a previous visit to Kwadwo's hometown. It turned out that she happened to be residing not very far from where I lived.

One day she came for a visit. Initially our conversation revolved around issues of general interest—our last meeting in the village, my friendship with Kwadwo, about my education and my plans for the future.

Then came the surprising moment! Turning to me, she asked unexpectedly: "Have you already given your life to Jesus the Lord?"

I was startled by her question and, for a moment, I was lost for words. "Well", I replied thoughtfully, choosing my words carefully, "I can't say I understand what you mean by that. I'm not an atheist. I do indeed believe in God. I do not attend church regularly, however."

"My question is", she said, "have you made a conscious decision to follow the Lord? It is not enough to go to church from time to time. I also used to attend church from time to time. But I was still living a wild life—until I got to know the Lord. Now I am free, free, free!" She smiled. "As the scriptures put it, 'If the Son makes you free you will be free indeed!' Another scripture says: 'God so loved the world that He sent His only begotten son, that whoever believes in Him will not perish but have eternal life.'" She smiled and looked at me expectantly.

I looked at her in bewilderment. For the moment I thought I wasn't hearing her correctly. Though I couldn't call myself an *active* Christian, I had quite a good knowledge of scripture. The thought that went through my mind as I sat face-to-face with her was of the nature: "Is Saul also among the prophets?" She might have read my thoughts.

"Well", she went on, "I know for sure that Kwadwo and the others have told you something about me—in particular in regard to the wild life I used to live!"

She smiled, but her words were serious. "Indeed, in former times I lived to please the flesh. I allowed my flesh to dictate my actions. I was a wretched sinner, used by the Devil the way he wanted. But recently things came to a head in my life. Indeed, I went through a severe crisis."

She took in my look of surprise. "Oh yes, my life seemed for ever shattered. Just at that moment God, through mysterious circumstances, came to call me. I obeyed the call and gave my Life to Jesus the Lord. Now I am free, free, free!"

She continued her testimony for a while. She spoke eloquently about her newfound hope, from time to time quoting scripture to stress her point. Her eyes sparkled with joy as she spoke—a joy not feigned. I sensed her genuine happiness that radiated from deep inside her.

Finally, she turned to look me in the eye: "I am inviting you to accept Jesus into your life. I have heard from Kwadwo and others that you are a brilliant scholar. Give your life to the

Lord Jesus and He will use you to His glory." She smiled but again spoke earnestly. "Oh indeed! You will never regret your decision to follow the Rock of Ages! If the Lord can change someone like me, He can do the same with you." She paused for breath, then continued: "Please give some thought to what you have heard. The Bible says in Revelation 3:20: 'Behold, I stand at the door and knock; if any man hear my voice and open the door, I will come into him, and will sup with him, and he with me.' Today may be your last chance! I don't know whether you worship in any church at all. In any case I want to invite you to worship with us on Sunday. I could pass here on my way to church to call on you."

Once again, I was lost for words. Eventually I found my tongue. "You really want me to worship with you?"

"Oh indeed! The congregation will be glad to welcome you."

"What kind of church is it?"

"It is known as the Open Bible Church."

"Open Bible Church?"

"You have never heard of the Open Bible Church?"

"No."

"Well, it is a Pentecostal Church—a truly Bible-based church. You may come and see things for yourself!"

"You'll have to give me time to digest all that you've told me today!"

"Don't harden your heart, my dear! Today is the day of your salvation; tomorrow may be too late."

"Will you please give me some time to think about it?"

Not long afterwards she begged to leave—but, before she left, she asked me to join her in a short prayer.

She prayed that the Lord would open my heart and help break the last resistance remaining in me. I accompanied her to the gate of the house.

Grace's testimony would not give me rest on my return. That she of all people would be the one to talk to me about salvation! I had heard and read about the transforming power of scripture. I did not need to search for a living testimony of those assertions—for Grace indeed was an embodiment of that testimony!

Just at that moment my eyes caught sight of my Methodist hymn book. It happened to be lying on one corner of the writing desk. Even to this day I cannot explain why I decided to pick it up. The moment I got hold of it, behold, it opened up at Hymn 157, the only hymn marked in the book, the hymn that had spoken to my heart so powerfully a few months before at the funeral at Mfantsipim.

The lines stared at me in my face:

Jesus Calls us! Over the tumult
of our life's wild restless sea,
Day by day His sweet voice
soundeth
Saying: Christian follow me.

As of old, apostles heard it
By the Galilean lake,
Turned from home and toil and
kindren
Leaving all for His dear sake.

Jesus calls us from the worship
Of the vain world's golden store,
From each idol that would keep us,
Saying: Christian love Me more!

In our joys and in our sorrows,
Days of toil and hours of ease,

Still He calls, in cares and pleasures,
That we love Him more than these.

Jesus calls us! By thy mercies,
Saviour, make us hear Thy call
Give our hearts to Thine obedience.
Serve and Love Thee best of all.

I read through the whole hymn, verse by verse. I reread it a second time. Goose-pimples formed all over my body as I went through the lines. For a while I could hardly control my tears.

Grace's testimony alone might not have been enough to move my stony heart. That sign—the hymn—following so closely on the heels of her touching testimony served as the proverbial last straw that was needed to break the back of the camel.

"The Lord has found you at last", a still voice within me seemed to say. "In the past you did not heed the call. This time there is nowhere you can run to."

An unusual quiet filled the room. Without knowing what I was doing I was on my knees, praying.

When I got up, I looked out for a Bible. There were a couple of them in the room. I got hold of one and began to read from a passage in the New Testament. All of a sudden, the words began to speak to my heart in a manner that I had not experienced before. I contacted Grace the next day to let her know about my willingness to accompany her to church the following Sunday. As expected, she was delighted at the news! We arranged for her to pass by my home on her way to church.

Together we would drive on a Tro-Tro (the name given to commuter buses in Ghana) to the church which was located about three miles away.

I accompanied her to church the following Sunday as planned. The church service began around 10 in the morning

17

with praise and worship. This was followed by Sunday School, which took about 45 minutes. At last, the sermon was delivered and the session ended around 2 in the afternoon.

Pastor Ofosu-Mensah delivered a touching sermon on my first visit. At the end of the service, he made the altar call. I did not hesitate a minute in heeding the call. Eventually I and a few others were invited to go forward to the altar to be prayed for.

After he had prayed for us, he congratulated us on our decision. Amid cheerful applause and shouts of "Welcome home! Welcome home!" we returned to our seats.

4

The dream of promise

Behold, the former things are come to pass, and new things do I declare: before they spring forth I tell you of them.

Isaiah 42:9 (KJV)

Background

I n the previous chapter I narrated the events leading to my conversion. As already mentioned, at the time of my conversion I had just completed my GCE A levels. My wish as I wrote my exams was to pass well in my exams and gain admission to medical school in Accra.

Why did I want to study medicine?

Well, my desire to study medicine was hatched at the time I was growing up in the small village with the big name!

The human suffering I was exposed to as a child played a not insignificant role to influence my decision. The nearest hospital was located about 20 miles away. The population was made up of poor peasants. As a result of the widespread poverty, residents sought medical help at the hospital only as a last resort.

Even if they managed to gather the money needed to pay for their transportation and to meet the expected hospital bills, the means of transporting the sick could be a problem, for the road leading from Mpintimpi to Nkawkaw where the hospital is located was less frequented by traffic at that time.

The villagers were small-scale farmers. They grew what they ate and ate what they grew. Accompanying the sick to hospital could cost them a whole day's work on their farms. They could not boast of any government agency that would compensate for the loss.

As a result, those who fell ill tended, before seeking conventional medical treatment, to wait at home and try traditional medicines until their condition deteriorated. In some cases, it was too late for them to be helped!

This and various other adverse factors that negatively influenced the provision of healthcare to the population influenced my decision to study medicine. I wanted to make a difference. I dreamt of operating a clinic on wheels, with which I would drive around the neighbourhood to provide healthcare to the community.

Literally on fire for the Lord in the immediate aftermath of my conversion, and burning with enthusiasm to work in the service of my Master, Jesus the Lord, I was faced with two options—to go straight to Bible School and become a pastor, or first to realise my previously cherished goal of becoming a doctor, after which I would serve the Lord in whichever capacity He found appropriate.

In the end I decided on the second option, for the following reason—I did not want to be a financial burden to the church I would pastor (if any) in the future. Of course, I have nothing against pastors being paid by their churches for their services. Personally, however, I was fascinated by the example of Apostle Paul who worked as a tentmaker partly to support himself, not wanting to overburden the young churches that he founded.

Neither did we eat any man's bread for nought; but wrought with labour and travail night and day, that we might not be chargeable to any of you: Not because we have not power, but to make ourselves an ensample unto you to follow us. For even when we were with you, this we commanded you, that if any would not work, neither should he eat.

1 Thessalonians 3:8–10

So I prayed the Lord to help me to make it to medical school. I beseeched Him, as it were, first to help me earn a trade, after which I would use my training to further His Kingdom. I knew the Lord had endowed me with the mental capability to study medicine. What I was lacking was the financial backing. The prevailing educational policy of the country favoured me, though; not only was tuition free up to university level, the state also provided free accommodation and free boarding to students. As if that were not enough, students could also access generous loans guaranteed by the state for the acquisition of textbooks and other educational material

As I mentioned earlier, Grace, who led me to Christ, lived not very far from me. By virtue of living close to each other, we interacted with each other on a regular basis—we took the same commuter bus to church, met for prayer and bible study, went shopping together, etc. In the course of time she revealed to me her immediate plans for the future. Her brother was resident in Germany. Her sister-in-law, who had developed a liking for her, was planning to invite her for a visit to Europe. Her hope was that, whilst there, she might be able to settle there for a while.

About two weeks after my conversion, when I was literally on fire for the Lord, I experienced my first disappointment in my Christian life—it concerned my A-Level results. Although I passed in all four subjects, my performance fell short of what I thought I was capable of achieving. Indeed, I failed to attain the first class results I had expected, the grades that would have catapulted me straight into one of the two medical schools in the country.

In the end, the university offered me admission to pursue a course in General Science. Though I accepted the offer, I considered it a stop-gap measure, a kind of plan B whilst I worked towards the attainment of plan A.

Just as I was struggling to come to terms with the unexpected turn of events in my academic pursuit, in October 1978 I came into contact with a good acquaintance of mine. On hearing the story of my failure to obtain admission to medical school in Ghana, he promised to use his good connections with the Ghana–Soviet Friendship Society to help get me a scholarship to study medicine in the Soviet Union.

The selection was due at the beginning of January 1979; he would do all he could to ensure I became a beneficiary of one of the several scholarships placed at the disposal of the organisation by the Soviet Union, he assured me.

By way of a short explanation: This was the era of the Cold War. The countries of the then Eastern Bloc placed at the disposal of countries of the developing world—from Africa, South America and Asia—hundreds of scholarships to enable their citizens to study in their countries. The scholarships were allegedly offered without any strings attached. At the back of the minds of the donors was, of course, the hope that the beneficiaries, after their long stay in their donors' societies, would return to propagate the communist ideology in their various countries.

Though it was clear to me I might not find other Christians to fellowship with whilst in the communist country, I was nevertheless keen on pursuing that path to medical school. I was convinced if it was His will to send me to the Soviet Union, He would also preserve my faith during my stay.

At the time I made the conscious decision to follow the Lord, I was not baptised. A few days before Christmas 1978, together with a group of other church members, I underwent water baptism at a popular beach, the Labadi beach, in Accra.

Bubbling with the fire and enthusiasm of a young convert, I decided to dedicate the period between Christmas and the New Year to a period of fasting and prayer.

On one such day, after a long night of prayer, I retired to bed. Was I really asleep or was I half-awake? One thing I am aware of, I was not fully conscious. Suddenly a scene flashed before my eyes—it was so vivid that even to this day I can very clearly recall it!

In the dream I happened to be walking on the street of a settlement that, from the setting, looked like any other town in Ghana. Just as I wandered on the street, all of a sudden the sister who led me to Christ emerged from nowhere. Surprised at seeing me, she exclaimed at the top of her voice:

"Peprah! So at long last we have met in EUROPE!"

Just then I came back to myself. I looked around me—all was deep silence. The walls of the room became familiar. It dawned on me that I had been in a dream.

Such a revelation, coming in a period of fasting and prayer, convinced me beyond all doubt that it was the Lord, who knows the beginning from the end, pointing future events to me.

How could my sister and I meet in Europe? I began to conjecture—as far as my Sister-in-Christ was concerned, her sister-in-law, a German citizen, was making the necessary arrangements to help her to settle in Germany. She had promised not only to help her obtain a visa, but also to bear the costs of her flight.

On my part, I speculated that I would be studying in the Soviet Union. My understanding was that foreign students were permitted to travel to the West during holidays. I would take advantage of the opportunity and travel to Germany to visit my sister; in that way, I presumed, the prophecy would be fulfilled.

It did indeed seem as if the prophecy would be fulfilled in the way I thought, for I was initially selected for the Soviet scholarship. My joy was beyond bounds. The plan was that the successful candidates, about two dozen in number, would leave for the Soviet Union in August that year.

Just as I had become accustomed to the idea of leaving Ghana later in the year to study in the Soviet Union, news reached me, about six weeks after my selection, that my name had been dropped from the list! One can imagine how disappointed I was at the news!

I did not want to accept the decision without a fight, though. Indeed, over the next several days, I contacted many leading members of the Ghana-Soviet Friendship Society, including the national president, to plead my case. But to no avail.

Just as things seemed to be going against me, matters were proceeding favourably on the part of my Christian sister. After some initial challenges, she finally managed to join her relations in Germany in February 1980.

For a while there seemed to be no way for the prophecy in the dream of meeting my sister on the streets of Europe coming to fulfilment. My sister was in Germany, but I was stuck in Accra. My dream of studying medicine also seemed to have been shattered.

Just as I was giving up hope of the prophecy becoming a reality, I bumped into Gyasi. I had got to know him during a visit to the hometown of Kwadwo, who, as readers might recall, was my best friend and classmate at secondary school. The last time I met him he was also doing his Sixth Form. At that time he spoke about his desire to study architecture after obtaining his GCE A-levels.

During our meeting he made it known to me that he would be leaving for Nigeria in the next few days. His plan was to look for work in Lagos, Nigeria's capital, to enable him to obtain his air ticket to join his brother in the US. His ultimate goal was to study architecture there.

I decided to accompany him to Nigeria. On my part, I would work to finance my journey to Germany with the goal of realising my goal of studying medicine.

Grace who was in the meantime settled in Hamburg, promised to do what she could to help me should I make it there.

On my arrival in Nigeria, initially I was forced to perform odd jobs on various construction sites to earn a living. Eventually I found employment as a pupil teacher.

After working in Nigeria for about 18 months, I saved enough money to enable me to book a flight to what was then East Berlin. From there I moved on to West Berlin. My plan to continue straight on to Hamburg could not be immediately realised. It was during the time of the Cold War when Germany was divided into the communist East and the capitalist West. As a result of West Berlin's peculiar status as a capitalist enclave in communist East Germany, I needed a visa to travel from West Berlin to my sister in Hamburg in West Germany. Without such a visa I had no choice but to remain in West Berlin.

Still desirous of realising my goal of becoming a doctor, I made the necessary inquiries as to the requirements for admission to medical school in Germany. In so doing I learnt that the chance of a foreigner like myself gaining admission to medical school was virtually nil. Despite my poor prospects, I was not dismayed. Instead, my resolve was strengthened to work towards achieving the almost impossible. Most importantly, I made serious efforts to study the German language. Because I did not have the financial means to attend a language school, I ended up teaching myself the language.

My effort was not in vain. Indeed, contrary to all expectations, the Hanover Medical School offered me admission in October 1983—but because of my status as an asylum seeker, the immigration authorities refused to grant me permission to travel from West Berlin to Hanover to commence my studies.

As one might imagine, I was shattered by the news. In the midst of this bleak situation, a glimmer of hope appeared on the horizon—the university promised to give me a second chance the following year.

The university kept its promise. This time I managed to travel from West Berlin to register for my studies. Eventually I matriculated at the medical school in October 1984.

On my way from East Berlin to Hanover, I made a detour to Hamburg on September 4, 1984, to pay a visit to my sister in Hamburg. Thus, almost six years after the prophecy was revealed to me, we *met on the streets of Europe!*

I have told the story as it happened. The Lord I serve knows I have not added anything to my account.

I must stress that the prophesy was not fulfilled in an easy manner. Indeed, on several occasions along the way, the obstacles, challenges, difficulties seemed insurmountable; the circumstances seemed to overwhelm me to the extent that I was often tempted to give up.

Almighty God, who knows the end from the beginning, had however spoken, and there were no human obstacles and impediments that could prevent His will from happening, as long as I maintained my faith—to His Name be the honour and glory forever and ever.

5

Through medical school with a mere €1000

My God shall supply all your need according to his riches in glory by Christ Jesus.

Philippians 4:19 (KJV)

In October 1984, I matriculated as a first-year student of the Hanover Medical School. Prior to that I had spent around two and a half years in West Berlin. During my time in that city I worked occasionally as a cleaner. I managed to save 2000 DM from my earnings. This works out at around 1020 Euros. That was all the financial resources at my disposal at the time I began my studies.

Then, as now, tuition is free in German universities for both citizens and non-citizens. Though they are not charged for teaching/lessons, students have to bear the cost of accommodation, food, books and other miscellaneous costs associated with their studies.

At the time I began my studies, it was generally held that students required around 700 German marks (about 360 Euros) monthly to sustain themselves. Based on that figure, I had at the outset enough money to last me barely three months.

Despite this, I was neither panicky nor apprehensive as to how to make it financially. Indeed, I trusted Almighty God, who had brought me all the way from my small village in Africa to medical school in Germany, to supply all my needs. In the end He did indeed supply my needs abundantly, indeed far beyond what I could imagine!

Let me now provide a roll call of the individuals, institutions and organisations the Lord used to help me through medical school:

American Lutheran Church in Berlin: During my stay in Berlin, I worshipped with the American Lutheran Church in Berlin. Earlier on in my stay I came across a leaflet of theirs inviting visitors to the city to worship with them. I called Gary, the pastor, who gave me directions to the church. I remained with them for the rest of my stay in the city.

Not long after my arrival in Hanover, Gary informed me the congregation had decided to assist me financially with a stipend of 300 DM every quarter.

Kurt and Karen: Kurt was the pastor of a German Lutheran church, which happened to be a sister church of the American Lutheran Church. Occasionally we held joint church services. It was during one such meetings that I got to know him.

Kurt played a key role in my university application process by providing a written declaration of financial support in case I gained admission—it was a vital piece of paperwork that I needed to provide before any university would consider my application.

On my admission, Kurt decided, in effect, to put his money where his mouth was! Not long after my arrival in Hanover, I received a letter from him in which he had enclosed a cheque for 400 DM. That was only the beginning, he stated. Together with his wife Karen, he announced, they had decided, until further notice, to support me with a monthly remittance of 200 DM.

Ilse: A Christian physiotherapist I got to know during my stay in hospital following surgery on my left ankle. Readers may recall I referred to this problem earlier on. The condition flared up during my first winter necessitating surgery. Alone in hospital, far away from home, I found comfort from reading through Scripture. That attracted her to me. Indeed, she was flabbergasted to find anyone with the courage to read the Bible in public—a revelation that on my part sent shockwaves through my spine and left me wondering why something that wouldn't raise an eyebrow in my native Ghana did so in Germany. That meeting came as a blessing. In the end she introduced me to several German Christians who also became a blessing to me. Ilse supported me with regular contributions of 100 DM.

Rhea: A retired Christian doctor I got to know through Ilse, who sent me monthly contributions of 100 DM.

Friedo: He was a pastor of a Lutheran Church in Hanover. He happened to be a good acquaintance of Kurt. Kurt established the contact with Friedo on my move to Hanover. In the end Friedo's church supported me with 100 DM monthly.

Gottfried: My first address in Hanover was in Langenhagen, a suburb of the city. By virtue of that, Friedo connected me to Gottfried, who happened to be the superintendent pastor responsible for the Langenhagen area of the German Lutheran Church in the city.

Gottfried and his wife Sabine welcomed me wholeheartedly to their home.

"You can consider yourself part of our family. In the worst-case scenario if you are unable to pay your rent, you can come and lodge with us!" they assured me.

In the end, Gottfried came up with a plan—he opened an account for me and launched an appeal for help from members of his congregation as well as his numerous acquaintances and associates. From that account he made a monthly payment of 200 DM to support me.

Anonymous donor: For a long time I received a substantial amount of money every month from an anonymous source. Eventually I got to know the source—a member of Gottfried's congregation. He did not want "the whole world to know" he was helping me, which is why he chose the anonymous route— so he told me.

Earnings from translation jobs: As if all the help I was getting through His grace were not enough!!

One day, not long after I had begun my studies, I was contacted by the head of the foreign students' office of the medical school. The police, I was told, were desperate to find someone who could translate from Twi, my native language. They had arrested a woman who was trying to enter the country on what they believed was a forged Ivory Coast passport. Contrary to the experience they had had with other Ghanaians, this particular individual did not understand any European language. With the deadline they were legally permitted to keep her locked up without a charge fast approaching, they desperately needed to find a translator for her.

I obliged and accepted the invitation.

At the end of my duty the officer preparing the invoice inquired about my rate.

"I have no idea", I replied.

"Well, Twi, your native language is classified as an exotic language; it therefore attracts a high rate. The translator we usually work with charges 70 DM per hour. He is a certified translator though. In your case, you are entitled to 50 DM per hour."

I just could not believe my ears at what I was hearing! At that point in time, the minimum wage was below 10 DM per hour. I really doubted that even my lecturers earned that much! An ordinary student earning an hourly rate comparable to that of a lecturer, if not higher! I could only thank the Lord for His favour.

That first translation job opened a door of opportunity for me, serving as an important additional source of income. Indeed, over the next several years, I received on quite a regular basis translation offers not only from the police but other authorities—the courts, immigration, those charged with the processing of asylum applications, etc.

When I got to the third year, the mysterious hands of God led me to an even more secure source of income—I was granted a scholarship by the Fredrich Ebert Foundation, which was affiliated to the German Social Democratic party. It was a scheme designed to help foreign students and had little to do with politics.

At that stage I dispatched a "thank you" note to the individuals and churches that had been supporting me, informing them about the new development and requesting they withdraw their support.

Through the mysterious workings of Almighty God, the poor student that I was at the commencement of my studies became very well provided for.

A good friend of mine, an Iranian of the Muslim faith, who was aware of the support I was receiving, one day looked me in the eye and began: 'Hey, Robert, your Jesus is very generous to you! He seems indeed to be giving you everything you ask Him for!'

"Well, you have yourself noticed how magnanimous He is! Accept Him into your life and He will do the same if not even greater things for you."

"You want to make me a Christian?" He shook his head. "No, I believe in our prophet, in Mohammed!"

I have not ceased praying for him, that he will come and taste and see the goodness of the Lord.

31

6

A very present help in time of need

God is our refuge and strength, a very present help in trouble.

Therefore will not we fear, though the earth be removed, and though the mountains be carried into the midst of the sea;

Though the waters thereof roar and be troubled, though the mountains shake with the swelling thereof. Selah.

Psalm 46: 1–3 (KJV)

While a student in Germany, one of my German mates invited me to his wedding at his hometown, about 60 miles from Hanover where I was resident. I planned my journey in such a manner as to arrive at my destination about an hour prior to the church service.

I travelled in a rented car. The vehicle was barely six months old, so I was confident it would get me to my destination without developing any mechanical problems. Nevertheless, I was about 20 minutes' drive from my destination when I heard a strange noise emanating from the back of the vehicle! I pulled to a stop on the relatively quiet road. I realised to my dismay that one of the back tyres was punctured.

I was sure the almost new vehicle would have on board a spare tyre as well as the tools needed to change the damaged tyre. At that moment in my life, however, I had no idea how to do that! Thankfully God, who provides ever-present help in times of trouble, was aware of my predicament, even before it happened and had dispatched help for my rescue.

Indeed, just as I got out of my vehicle, another vehicle coming from the direction I was heading towards arrived at the scene. On seeing my problem, the driver pulled to a stop.

"That is one of the unfortunate things that can happen to a driver!" he began.

"Yes indeed, particularly so when you are a few kilometres from your destination!" I replied.

"May I help you fix the problem?"

"That is most kind of you! To be honest with you, I have no idea how to do it!"

Soon he went to work to change the damaged tyre. He could indeed be counted among the experts—for he completed the assignment in no time at all.

"Goodbye and safe journey!" He shook my hand and made for his vehicle. Moments later he was out of sight.

Through this timely intervention, I reached my destination in time for the celebrations.

My friend was proud of his African friend. He wanted me to be part of the celebrations, for I would, as he saw it, provide an international flare to what would otherwise have been a purely German affair. I just cannot imagine how disappointed he would have been had I been late for the service, or had I missed it entirely!

Indeed, Almighty God is a present help in times of trouble, so let us not be overcome by fear of what tomorrow might bring.

7

When you pass through fire it will not burn you

When thou passest through the waters, I will be with thee; and through the rivers, they shall not overflow thee. When thou walkest through the fire, thou shalt not be burned, neither shall the flame kindle upon thee.
Isaiah 43:2 (KJV)

The incident I am about to narrate, the recollection of which has sent goose-pimples running all over my body, happened about 35 years ago, at a time when I was a second-year student at the Hanover Medical School in Germany. Though it happened several years ago, it is still fresh in my memory.

At that time I was resident in one of the three hostels built in and around the medical school compound to provide accommodation for part of the student population. In the case of two of the three hostels, each tenant had a small room that contained a bath and toilet facilities. The rooms were not fitted with kitchen facilities, however. Instead, each floor was equipped with a spacious kitchen boasting several electric stoves as well as some refrigerators where residents of that particular floor could cook their meals and also store their food items.

The third hostel, the one in which I stayed, was built differently. It was made up of several small flats each boasting two bedrooms, a small furnished living room leading to both rooms, a small built-in kitchen at one corner of the living room as well as a small enclosure adjacent to the kitchen equipped with a shower and WC.

When I moved into the flat, a German student named Roland occupied one of the bedrooms. As I learnt later from him, he had switched to medicine after having almost completed a degree course in physics and mathematics. Each of the two bedrooms had a plug-in socket for a telephone.

This meant that I could apply for my own telephone number. To save money, however, we decided to share the one already being used by my flatmate. Today, in the age of the mobile phone, none of us would have thought of applying for a landline. But this was 1984—I personally had not heard about mobile phone technology at that point in time!

Roland demonstrated his skills in mathematics in a practical way by coming up with a complicated formula by which he calculated the percentage of the monthly phone bill each of us had to be responsible for, based on the line rental and the actual units used.

My custom was to eat at the students' canteen during the week, and prepare my own meals at the weekend. In most cases I prepared fufu, which, without doubt, is the most popular Ghanaian dish. For the sake of those not familiar with that meal, I shall pause to offer a short description.

At home in Ghana the meal is prepared by first pounding boiled plantains together with cassava in a wooden mortar. In the process a thick elastic carbohydrate ball is obtained. Ghanaians in the so-called diaspora, especially those living in the West, usually substitute the two main ingredients, plantain and cassava, with powdered potato and powdered starch respectively. In this case the two ingredients are stirred in boiled water for a while to obtain a product of a similar consistency, like that of the original fufu balls.

Fufu balls are swallowed by means of soup. The soup can be prepared in various ways—by means of palmnut or groundnut cream, or one can prepare so-called "light soup" by making use of tomato paste together with some pepper. Meat, fish or a mixture of both are usually added to the soup at some stage in the preparation.

One Saturday after I had prepared a delicious fufu meal, I decided to keep part of the soup in the fridge to be used for another meal the following day. As was my custom, I attended church the next day. On my return at around 2 in the afternoon, I set about to prepare another meal of fufu. After stirring the potato and starch into a ball, I removed the soup from the previous day from the fridge, warmed it and poured part into a bowl.

After enjoying my meal, I realised there was still enough soup left for one more meal! I decided therefore to keep it in the fridge for another occasion. It was still hot, however, so I resolved to allow it to cool down before placing it back into the fridge.

Soon after the meal I began to feel tired. I decided therefore to retire to my room, not primarily with the intention of sleeping, but of resting for a while. As I mentioned earlier on, it was a Sunday afternoon. Roland, like the majority of residents in the hostel, had travelled home for the weekend. He was not expected until late in the evening.

Before long, the heavy meal took its toll, and soon I was overtaken by sleep. What I did not realise before retiring to my bed was that I had failed to switch off the electric stove on which the soup was still standing!

As I lay down sleeping, knocked out, as it were, by the heavy meal, the electric stove was faithfully working to supply heat to boil the soup placed upon it. While danger was thus growing in the living room, the man of flesh that I am was deeply asleep; not only sleeping, but perhaps also snoring loudly!

Though asleep, the electric mains were not! The effect was that initially all the water in the soup evaporated. Soon the solids contained in it—meat, fish, vegetables—began to bear the full brunt of the energy being delivered. In the course of time, they began to burn, sending fumes to fill the living room.

For reasons that I cannot even now explain, I had shut the door to my bedroom before making for my bed. Since there was hardly any space between the carpeted floor and the door, I was spared the fumes. Not so the main door to the flat. The fumes escaped through the space underneath it to fill the corridors of the third floor of the building where my room was located.

If it had been a working day, when much going and coming usually took place in the hostel, someone almost certainly would have detected the fumes. Roland might also have been around.

However, it was a Sunday afternoon—Roland and the majority of the residents of the hostel were away. Thus, when I needed help the most, no human being was around to offer me any help—to draw my attention to the impending danger.

So on that fateful afternoon, several years ago, as I lay snoring in my bed, and the soup on the electric stove in the forecourt of my room was burning with red hot flames and nearing the point of exploding to set the room, and possibly the whole building, on fire, the whole of the world had in effect deserted me.

The question one may ask is—was there no fire alarm system in place in the room? Well, it was a huge building made up of several storeys. Certainly, there were alarm systems installed at some points in the building—and yet not in our room.

Thank God, heaven does not need a man-made fire alarm system to be alerted about fire raging in our homes. For sure, omnipotent and omnipresent God is there wherever His children are and is ever ready to despatch His angels to rescue them from danger.

Just as I lay snoring in my bed, completely unaware of the impending danger, as the fire was raging on in the flat, before it was too late, the Lord my Shepherd activated a rescue plan in heaven to deliver me—unworthy me—from danger!

Indeed, before it was too late, all of a sudden I heard, as if in a dream, the sound of the ringing of a phone. Soon I came back to myself. It dawned on me that it was our phone that was ringing. I sprang out of my bed and headed for it. The scary scene that met my eyes on opening the door is still vivid before my eyes! Not only was the dish burning with red hot flames, the whole living room was filled with thick smoke!

With a sense of shock written all over my face, I rushed to the stove and switched it off. Next, I pulled the burning dish from the stove and placed it in the washbasin. Hardly able to find my way because of the thick smoke, I picked up the phone that was still ringing.

"I want to speak to Roland", the caller began after the initial greetings.

"He has travelled home for the weekend."

"Tell him his friend Peter called. Let him know that I misplaced his number; that is why I have not called him for a while. I just chanced upon it as I was putting my room in order. I decided to try it, to find out whether he is still using it."

"That is fine: I will let him know you called."

After I had put the receiver back in place, I began to ponder on the conversation. To the caller, it had just seemed a matter of chance that he came across his friend's lost telephone number and called him. In the economy of the God of Heaven and Earth, however, there is nothing like chance, dear friends. I do believe that it was the Lord my Shepherd, the Sure Refuge in trouble, the Most High and Loving God who moved him to call when he did, so as to make me aware of the imminent threat to my life.

8

From the Sovereign Lord comes escape from death

Our God is a God who saves; from the Sovereign LORD comes escape from death.

Psalm 68:20 (NIV)

In the summer of 2007, my wife Rita and I, together with our three children, visited our native Ghana. All our children were born in Hanover and the journey offered them the opportunity of visiting the land of their parents for the first time.

After visiting my family at Mpintimpi, a small village about 100 miles to the northwest of Accra, we continued to Mim, Rita's hometown. On its part, Mim is situated about 240 miles to the northwest of Accra.

After spending two weeks with Rita's relations, we ended our journey and headed south. Our ultimate destination was Accra, to embark on our return flight to the UK. Our plan was to make a stopover in Kumasi, Ghana's second largest city, about 90 miles to the southeast of Mim, to visit my doctor friend Kwasi before heading back to Accra for our return journey to the UK.

The road we drove on was a single lane. Though the topography was generally flat, a few miles stretch of road led through rough mountainous terrain with curves and hairpin bends at several places. After about half an hour's drive through low-lying countryside displaying the typically green tropical vegetation, the landscape began gradually to change. Instead of flat land, several hills and mountains came into view. Corresponding with the changed landscape, the road we were travelling on, which had been straight and low-lying for the most part, increasingly began to display winding bends and arduous ascents as well as steep slopes.

Eventually we came to the bottom of a steep decline that preceded a steep rise. To facilitate the flow of traffic heading for the steep climb, the road, which so far had been a single carriageway, had been broadened at the base of the climb to become a dual carriageway for traffic heading towards the mountain. The dual carriageway applied only to ascending traffic.

Traffic down the slope was still by way of a single track or lane. Contrary to the situation on several roads in the country, this particular stretch of the road was visibly marked. Two bold continuous white markings were in place to underscore the need for traffic in each direction to keep to its lane. Also clearly visible were several white arrows painted on the road to indicate the direction of traffic.

Ours was the only vehicle on the road as we began the steep climb. After driving on it for a while, I realised we were heading for a bend about a hundred yards away. The vegetation at that part of the road was thick, making it difficult to see beyond it. Instinctively I had all along kept to the middle lane, which happened to be a direct extension of the lane I had all along been driving on. Barely a few yards before the bend, I instinctively decided to abandon the middle lane for the outside one. No sooner had I done so than I witnessed something that, to this day, continues to baffle my imagination. All of a sudden, and as if from nowhere, a large tipper truck emerged from the sharp bend a few yards ahead of us, driving—incredibly—in the middle lane, the lane that was absolutely out of bounds for traffic coming in that direction!

Even to this day, I cannot fathom what it was that led the driver to use that lane. His action was completely unprovoked.

There was no impediment in his way, he was not being hassled by any pursuing vehicle, and the lane earmarked for his use was completely free. So why did he choose to place the lives of others in such danger?

I just could not imagine what would have happened to us if I hadn't changed lanes just seconds before! One thing is certain, however—there would have been little chance of escape! I would probably have instinctively swerved to the side, lost control of the vehicle in the process, and been powerless to prevent it from rolling over several times down the steep slope and finally crashing into the valley below. Or, had I been left with no time to swerve, we might have crashed head on into the huge truck. It is anyone's guess what would have remained of a Mercedes mini-bus and its occupants after crashing into a truck not only of its size but against the momentum of its own mass, combined with the force of gravity pulling us down the steep slope.

I am more than convinced that we were being watched by Almighty God of Heaven, He whose eyes are able spontaneously to scan every corner of the universe at any given time, who is capable of seeing into the very minute detail of what is happening in every corner of Accra in Ghana, Canberra in Australia, Wuhan in China, Santiago de Chile in Chile—you can continue the roll call of every possible settlement on planet Earth until the cows come home!

The Omnipotent and Omnipresent God recognised the danger ahead of me and my family and dispatched one of His ever-willing angels to pull the vehicle out of danger.

"Pull the vehicle to the outside lane and out of danger!" the command was issued by the Ancient of Days! And in the twinkle of the an eye it was executed on Earth.

Almighty God is indeed our rock and shield, so we do not need to fear anyone.

9

An awesome gift from an unexpected source

And we know that all things work together for good to them that love God, to them who are called according to His purpose.

Romans 8:28 (KJV)

As already stated, in October 1984 I began my medical studies at the Hanover Medical School. Before moving to Hanover, I spent two years in the then West Berlin as an asylum seeker from Ghana. During my stay there, I worshipped at the American Lutheran Church in Berlin. It was during the Cold War. Germany was divided as a result of World War II. Several American soldiers were stationed in West Berlin. The American Lutheran Church was not part of the military establishment but rather served the English-speaking American civilian community as well as other English-speaking residents of the divided city from various parts of the globe.

After I had matriculated with the medical school of the northern German city, I applied for a room in one of the three hostels serving students registered with that institution of higher learning. Because there was no vacancy at that time, my name was placed on the waiting list. With the help of Pastor Kawalla, then the superintendent pastor of the German Lutheran Church for the Hanover-North district, I found temporary accommodation in a hostel serving mostly students of a theological seminary not far from the medical school. I learnt, on moving to my new accommodation, that not very far from the building was another facility that served as a refuge for delinquent teenagers who could no longer live with their parents.

To facilitate my movement and also to save the money I would otherwise have spent on going by public transport, I bought a new bicycle. My silver-coloured bike eventually became my good companion, enabling me to reach the lecture hall on time, helping me transport my shopping basket home and also taking me to the church where I worshipped, which happened to be located some 3 miles from the hostel. Like anyone else living in the hostel, I chained my bike every evening to a special stand that had been erected near the building for that purpose.

Barely three months after acquiring the bike, I left my room one morning to collect my bike for a ride to the medical school, not suspecting anything. I had, as usual, calculated my time so as to be punctual for lectures but, to my utter dismay, my faithful companion was nowhere to be seen! In my desperation I went about searching the compound around the building in the hope that perhaps someone had deposited it somewhere after using it for a riding tour. Apparently, someone among the delinquent teenagers had visited the stand during the night and made away with my good-looking bike.

At that time I belonged to a Bible study and prayer group led by Pastor Kawalla. One of the members of the group, on learning about my situation, presented me with a replacement. It was an old worn-out bike that could not in any way compare with the stolen one. Nevertheless, the fact that I had the means that could at least still make me independent of public transport was consoling enough for me.

A few days later, I rode it to church. With the help of a metal chain, I fastened it to a lamppost on the street a few yards from the church building. After a lively church service, I went to pick up the old bike for my ride home. What did I find? That one, too, was nowhere to be seen! I just couldn't believe my eyes! Why on earth would anyone want to steal anything like such an old bike?! So, two lost bikes within a period of less than two weeks! Somehow, I was tempted to be angry with God. In particular, the fact that I had lost the second bike while attending church was difficult for me to swallow.

But I was not someone who was new to the faith. Over a period of about 16 years to that day, I had experienced the working of the Great Redeemer in my life. Over that period of time He had turned several seemingly dead-end situations in my life around, in some instances in ways that were beyond my ordinary human understanding.

So, once the shock of my loss had abated and I stood there before the lamppost where I had fastened my bike a few hours earlier, I could only wonder what He had in store for me this time round!

But what was I to do? Although the city of Hanover boasts a well-functioning public transport service, commuter trains, streetcars, buses, etc., for the reasons already mentioned I preferred going by bike. My meagre financial resources would not permit me to buy a brand-new bike again. Even if I had the funds, the events of the last few days had made me reluctant to invest a substantial amount of money once again for that purpose.

In the end, acquiring another second-hand bike on the flea market was an alternative I was prepared to consider. Before I resorted to that, however, the idea occurred to me to call Gary, the pastor of the American Church in Berlin, to inform him of my predicament and request him to make an announcement in church the following Sunday, asking if there was any member of the church who might be ready to dispose of an old bike that was perhaps wasting away in the cellar or backyard of his or her home… Gary promised to do as requested.

A few days later I received a message from Berlin to the effect that one of the members of the church was willing to present me with a bike! Another member of the church who happened to be travelling to Hanover, a city located about 190 miles to the west of Berlin, agreed to bring it along.

The sight of the gift from Berlin has humbled me to this day. I was not being presented with an ordinary bike, but the type that in my opinion deserves the accolade "extraordinary"! It was a never used and elegant bright red-coloured six-gear sports bike! It may well have been worth three times the value of my first stolen bike. That anyone would be willing to part with it for free was beyond my comprehension.

The couple that donated it served with the US military in Berlin. They had brought the bike with them to Germany, thinking they would need it. That was, however, not the case. Their time in Berlin was just about to come to an end and they had been deliberating on how to dispose of it before their return home. They did not hesitate a moment after hearing the announcement to donate it to a person they had heard many good things about. I must say, though, that up to that time, they did not belong to the group of church members with whom I had close contact. For the next few days (and even up till now) the mysterious workings of the Lord that led me to the amazing bike has continued to baffle me and occupy my mind.

In the following years my bright red sports bike carried me over several hundred miles as I went about my daily life in the northern German city that boasted about half a million residents.

Whenever I ponder over the events that led me to the bike, the passage of scripture that comes to my mind is: "And we know that all things work together for good to them that love God, to them who are called according to his purpose."—Romans 8:28 (KJV)

10

The ageing Beetle that wouldn't take instructions!

The Lord will keep you from all harm—he will watch over your life; the Lord will watch over your coming and going both now and forevermore.

Psalm 121: 7–8

The city of Hanover where I attended medical school boasts a well-developed bicycle infrastructure. The public transportation system made up of buses and streetcars is also well developed and reliable.

At the time of my arrival in Europe, I did not have a driving licence. Partly because of the factors outlined above, and also because I did not have the time or the financial resources to invest in a driving school, the acquisition of a driving licence was not for a long while my top priority.

I arrived in Germany in 1982; in 1988 I returned to Ghana for the first time since my stay in Europe. During my stay, my senior brother taught me how to drive. In order not to "unlearn" or lose my driving skills on my return to Germany, I decided to keep up the momentum and acquire the German licence. After about six weeks of both theoretical and practical driving lessons, I acquired the driving permit in early 1989.

Though until then my bike had been conveniently taking me on my journeys through the city, I decided to acquire a small vehicle mainly with the goal of improving my driving skills. In the end I acquired a used Volkswagen Beetle for next to nothing.

One day I was driving home from lectures, driving along one of the main roads of the city. Trams travelled in the middle of the broad road along rails set into the street, with traffic flowing in opposite directions along each side of the tram lines. As I drove, a tram heading in the direction I was travelling sped past me. It came to a stop about 100 yards ahead of me. It was still at a standstill with the passengers alighting when I caught up with it.

I did not drive past it; I had to leave the main road to take a branch just before the tram stop. And so I left the main road turning into the branch road. The pedestrian traffic light just ahead of me, designed purposely for passengers heading to or away from the tram stop, was green for traffic.

Just a few yards before I could drive through the pedestrian crossing, the light turned red for traffic. About half a dozen pedestrians waiting for the green light, poured onto the road. I applied my brakes. Normally in dry conditions there was enough braking distance, which is the time between the application of the brakes and the vehicle coming to a stop. It had, however, just started to rain, causing the road surface to be slippery. As I had learnt in my driving school, such a condition not only increases the risk of skidding, it also increases the vehicle's braking distance.

And so, instead of obeying my orders to stop before the traffic light, conveyed through the pressing of the brakes on my part, the little red "metal cage" just carried on! Even to this day, I cannot fathom how everyone in the group managed to escape. Of course, sensing danger, each of them tried in their own respective way to escape the imminent danger. The fact that each one of them managed to escape the danger, to avoid being hit or knocked down by my vehicle, can aptly be described as miraculous, indeed beyond belief. Eventually, my vehicle came to a stop just yards beyond the traffic light.

Initially I thought some among the group would head for the vehicle to confront me. Happily, apart from a few of them staring at me and directing insulting gestures at me, they all walked away.

Some may be inclined to credit chance and/or luck for the favourable outcome of this incident. Nevertheless, as in the case of the near-miss accident involving our bus and the truck in Ghana, I am convinced it was Divine intervention that saved the day. It was by virtue of Almighty God dispatching a host of angels to my rescue, to pull each of the pedestrians to safety, that I was preserved from harm and trouble.

I would indeed have been in big trouble without His timely intervention!

My driving licence was issued on a two-year probation basis and, at that time, I was only a few months into my probation.

Even more serious consequences would have followed had any one of the bystanders there that day come to harm! It might have even resulted in the end of my studies! Indeed, had my vehicle run over and killed anyone, I may have been made to serve a long prison sentence for causing harm through reckless driving!

11

The angel of the Lord surrounding and defending me

*The angel of the LORD encampeth round about them
that fear him, and delivereth them.*
Psalm 34:7 (KJV)

A t one stage in my post-graduate training, I managed to
secure a job in a clinic in Bad Soden-Salmünster, a town
in the German Federal state of Hesse, about 220 miles to the
southwest of Hanover. I left home Sunday evenings and stayed
in rented accommodation and returned home on Friday
evenings.

As usual I headed home one Friday evening for the
weekend. After driving about an hour on a less busy road I
joined a busy highway connecting some major cities in the
area. After driving for a while on the busy highway, which had
four lanes heading each direction, the road went through
mountainous and undulating terrain with winding curves,
slopes and climbs alternating at short distances.

As might be expected on a Friday evening, the road was
busy with traffic, with commuters like myself working away
from home, heading home for the weekend. There was no
speed limit along that stretch of the highway. After driving in
the second lane for a while, I found myself behind a vehicle
driving at a slower speed than the average driver on the road.
To avoid the risk of collision, I decided to change to the third
lane.

Before carrying out the manoeuvre, I observed the traffic
behind me for a while through the rear-view mirror, to ensure it

was safe to do so. In so doing, I failed to take into consideration what I had learnt in my driving school about the blind spot, and the warning not to rely only on the rear-view mirror inside the car to observe traffic behind and around one's vehicle, but also to use the side mirror as well as turn the head and look over one's shoulder.

In any case I failed to take the additional precautions and went ahead and changed from the second to the third lane. In so doing I was not aware there was a vehicle just a few yards away from me in that lane!

Even today, I ask myself how the driver of that vehicle managed to avoid my vehicle by swerving quickly into the fourth lane, which, thankfully, had enough space to permit the manoeuvre!

I just could not imagine what would have happened if the vehicle had collided with mine. It would, without doubt, have resulted in a multi-vehicle collision of unimaginable proportions, leading with all certainty to multiple fatalities—including myself.

Sometimes I have the impression Almighty God has apportioned not only a single guarding angel, but legions of them, to take me through life!

12

A lone traveller and the scary wildlife

The Lord will guard your going out and your coming in
From this time forth and forever.

Psalm 121:8 (KJV)

I t was a chilly autumn morning. It was around 5:50 in the morning, still quite dark. I was driving along a dual carriage road in an isolated area of northern Germany. I was heading for a town about 90 miles to the west of Hanover for an appointment. I left early in the morning to be on time for the meeting.

That section of the road passed through a forest reserve. On each side of the highway there was no sign of human activity, just vegetation. Nature seemed to be at peace with herself.

I was alone in the vehicle; at that early hour of the day, the road was almost devoid of traffic. To keep me awake and also to follow world events, I had turned on the radio.

My thoughts were occupied with the day's busy schedule. After the meeting, I had to drive back to Hanover as quickly as possible to attend another meeting in the afternoon.

Then it happened! Without any warning, I heard a loud bang emanating from the front of the vehicle, from the driver's side! The huge impact caused the vehicle to spin and, for a moment, I thought I would lose control. Fortunately, I managed to keep the car under control and bring it to a stop.

Shocked beyond measure and at a loss to know what the matter was, I got out of the vehicle to investigate the cause of the impact. The sight of blood spillage on the road gave me a clue—a wildlife collision. I began to look around for the culprit. Soon I spotted the lifeless body of a deer on the hard shoulder, about fifty yards ahead of me. And what a huge deer it was!

Having established the cause of the problem, I set about inspecting the damage to the vehicle. One thing that struck me was the fact that a considerable amount of fuel was leaking out of the engine compartment, something that led me to think the engine had been damaged. This turned out to be the case.

Apart from that, there was substantial damage to the driver's side of the vehicle which had borne the brunt of the impact—the windscreen was also cracked.

Despite the damage, initially I thought I could start the engine and drive to the next available service station. But the engine failed to start.

In the end I called the German automobile club for assistance. With their help the vehicle was towed to the next available garage. I was provided with a courtesy car to enable me to continue my journey, just in time for my appointment.

As it turned out, the engine sustained considerable damage and needed to be replaced, together with several other components. The vehicle had comprehensive insurance cover so I did not have to worry about costs.

Speaking of insurance—whereas the vehicle had the benefit of worldwide insurance, indeed insurance cover that took care of the material damage, I counted on an even surer insurance— Divine protection. I have indeed read about several instances when vehicle collision with wildlife such as deer has led to loss of life of the driver and even other vehicle occupants.

13

Warding off demonic attacks in Jesus' name

No weapon that is formed against thee shall prosper; and every tongue that shall rise against thee in judgment thou shalt condemn. This is the heritage of the servants of the LORD, and their righteousness is of me, saith the LORD.

Isaiah 54:17 (KJV)

One day, whilst on a visit to my native Ghana in 2011, I began all of a sudden to experience a peculiar sensation in my head, a feeling difficult to put into words. It was a kind of burning sensation, of the type one experiences in the mouth after eating a hot spicy meal made with chilli pepper.

The burning sensation soon gave way to a kind of hotness, a hotness that engulfed not only the whole of my head, but also spread to the rest of my body. As if that were not enough, shortly after the onset of the weird symptoms I had a feeling as if someone was shaking my heart, causing it, as it were, to swing like a pendulum. Moments later my heart felt as if it were jumping to and fro in my chest, as one might feel on hearing an exciting bit of news. Soon my heart was not only "jumping around", but accelerating, accelerating rapidly.

The result of the abnormal activities of my heart was that, soon, I began to feel not only dizzy, but very bad indeed. Moments later I was barely able to keep my balance on the chair I was sitting on, as the whole world began to spin before my eyes!

Meanwhile I felt like collapsing to the floor. With all the strength I could muster, I made it to the bed a few yards away.

With my whole body feeling as if on fire, the world spinning before my eyes and beginning to experience some difficulty breathing, I felt for the first time in my life that I would probably not make it to the next day.

What was to be done?

I was in my native Ghana where the ambulance system was not well developed. Besides that, the hotel was far removed from the next available hospital. Furthermore, the main roads leading from the hotel were terribly congested for most of the day. I reckoned it would take me no less than an hour to get to the next available hospital, or the nearest hospital capable of providing any decent medical assistance—even if I were able to call the emergency services. In the meantime the weird symptoms worsened instead of improving.

At that moment, I decided to consult the only Doctor available at any time and place, the Greatest Physician of our age, the Best Help in time of trouble—the Doctor Who Knows No Bounds, He who is the same yesterday, today and forever more.

With all the strength left in me I began to pray: "Save me Lord Jesus, save me Lord Jesus; in your mighty Name, save me!" I recited those lines over and over again. I kept doing so for several minutes thereafter.

About half an hour after the onset of the symptoms I began to notice a gradual improvement in my condition. Both the hotness in the head and body reduced in intensity. My heart, while still beating fast, was not going as fast as before. Finally, about an hour after it all began, I felt strong enough to sit up on the bed.

The Lord is my shepherd, I shall not want ... though I walk through the valley of the shadow of death, I will fear no evil, for thou art with me; thy rod and thy staff they comfort me!"

Thus I encouraged myself with these words from Psalm 23.

After sitting for a while, I decided to lie down again. Soon I was overcome by sleep. When I woke up it was a few minutes past midnight, and the symptoms had disappeared. Indeed, I felt strong again.

I spent the next several minutes pondering my experience. The physician that I am, I just could not fathom what could be behind the weird set of symptoms I had just experienced. I had until then enjoyed excellent health. Indeed, I did not remember the last time in more than 25 years that I felt so sick that I had to stay away from lectures or work. Throughout my stay in Ghana, I had felt well. On that particular day, I had felt as fit as a fiddle.

So what was wrong with me? Indeed, I was at a loss as to the type of disease or condition that could result in the weird burning sensations in the brain.

A few days after the incident, I returned to the UK.

I thought the problem was behind me—but no, the problem recurred on not a few occasions.

On one such occasion, I happened to be at work in a prison. I had just taken my place behind my desk at the beginning of the afternoon clinic, which took off at 2 p.m., and was about to call my first patient when the familiar symptoms began again. I was subsequently sent to A&E in an ambulance!

A doctor one moment, a patient the next!

After undergoing various tests at A&E, I was discharged home after about six hours.

I began to wonder what the problem was with my heart. To get to the bottom of the matter, I went for extensive medical checks in Germany—which ruled out an organic cause. Put another way, the test failed to establish any physical changes in my body to explain the symptoms.

At that stage, I suspected something I had harboured all along—that I was under demonic attack, which I felt was now confirmed.

The battle lines were thus drawn: on one side Satan with his host of demons; and on the other side me, shielded by the Holy Spirit of the Ancient of Days.

The sister who led me to Christ once told me that Satan does not understand diplomatic language. According to her, the child of God needs to confront him aggressively—not in his or her own power, but shielded by the cross. That was exactly what I resolved to do. I was determined to carry the fight to the Devil, not by my might, but in the mighty Name of the Lord.

"Look here, demons", I declared, "I will not allow myself to be intimidated, no, never! In the Name of Jesus of Nazareth, depart from me and make for Hell, where you belong!" That was it! The enemy took to his heels and left me alone!

Indeed, more than eight years after making that declaration, I remain as fit as a fiddle. My heart has been dutifully pumping blood to perfuse my organs all this time. Not until He who brought me here calls me home, Lucifer dare not come near me!

(Those wishing to read a detailed account of this particular testimony may read my book *Warding Off Demonic Attacks in Jesus' Name*.)

14

When the Lord left a message on my laptop

In the same hour came forth fingers of a man's hand, and wrote over against the candlestick upon the plaister of the wall of the king's palace: and the king saw the part of the hand that wrote.

Daniel 5:5 (KJV)

I am sure some of my readers are familiar with this amazing Old Testament story of Divine intervention in world affairs. Those who wish to do so may read the whole account in Daniel 5.

I just want to provide a brief summary here.

Belshazzar, King of Babylon, organised a great feast for 1000 of his lords. During the feast, he commanded his servants to fetch the golden and silver vessels that his father, Nebuchadnezzar, had brought from the temple in Jerusalem to Babylon so the king, and his princes, his wives, and his concubines, might drink from them.

His command was followed. The king and his guests drank from them, praising their gods as they did so.

Then it happened! Suddenly a hand appeared from nowhere and began to write on the wall: "MENE, MENE, TEKEL, UPHARSIN" (Daniel 5:25 (KJV)). Not surprisingly, the king and everyone present were terrified, horror-stricken by the supernatural manifestation.

The king subsequently summoned his magicians and diviners and charged them with the task of interpreting the writing—but none of them could.

At that juncture the queen thought of Daniel, who was renowned for his wisdom. Daniel was accordingly called. The king asked him to help with the interpretation, promising to make him third in rank in the kingdom should he succeed in doing so. Daniel turned down the offer of promotion, but agreed to interpret the strange inscription all the same—not by his wisdom, he stressed, but rather through the wisdom imparted to him by Almighty God.

Daniel reminded Belshazzar that his father Nebuchadnezzar's greatness was the gift of God, and that when he became arrogant God threw him down until he learned humility: "…the Most High God has sovereignty over the kingdom of mortals, and sets over it whomever He will." Belshazzar had drunk from the vessels of God's Temple and praised his idols, but he had not given honour to God, and so God sent this hand and wrote those words:

"MENE, MENE, TEKEL, UPHARSIN"

What do they mean? "God had numbered his days, and had brought his reign to an end. His kingdom is divided and given to the Medes and Persians." Thus Daniel interpreted the inscription. That very night the king was slain and Darius the Mede took over the kingdom.

Many in our day discard such Biblical accounts for various reasons.

For some it is just a fairy-tale; just one of the Old Testament stories that should be taken with a pinch of salt. Some regard them as myths that should not be taken seriously, Still others regard them as folklores, legends that have no bearing to our day. Those who have such attitudes tend to harbour disdain for those who choose to believe them—considering them naïve, unsophisticated, simple-minded, unschooled, etc.

Well, if you are inclined to think that way, I urge you to pay attention as I narrate what I term a "writing on the wall" experience. I had such an experience, seeing with my own naked eye words from our Lord on Saturday April 25, 2020, at around 7:25 in the morning local time. Indeed, before my own eyes, the Lord left the message: "Wishes can never fill a sack" on a Microsoft Word document page of my laptop computer!

Making such a claim immediately raises the question of credibility. How credible is my account? Well, in the matter of credibility I want to say the following:

Concerning my person: I am an elderly man with grey hair and facial wrinkles. I shall not mention my real age for, after all, the date of my birth was not recorded. It will suffice to say that my age is based on the accounts of my parents who are no longer alive—but in general terms at the time of writing I have been here for just over six decades.

Concerning my faith: I made a conscious decision to follow the Lord Jesus in September 1978. Though by no means the perfect Christian I would like to be, by His grace, I have kept the faith.

Concerning my profession: In alphabetical order, I refer to myself as author, evangelist and medical doctor. I am not implying by any means that being a Christian doctor makes me infallible. I am not claiming to be faultless, flawless, error-free, the only angel in a world populated by imperfect human beings.

Finally—I am happily married to my wife Rita. We have three children.

Those who have been called to witness in court, those fulfilling high offices such as leaders of their countries, heads of the judiciary, attorney-generals etc., are often asked whether they want to swear on the sacred book of their religion, the Bible, the Koran, the Torah, etc. Should someone put such a question to me concerning the testimony I am about to give, I will answer without any hesitation in the affirmative. Indeed, I am prepared to swear on the Holy Bible to stress the fact that I am saying nothing but the truth.

Allow me to elaborate even further on the matter.

Admittedly, no human being apart from myself witnessed it. I was alone in my study. Rita and the rest of the family were still asleep. Though no human being was around to witness it, I was not alone. Two of the attributes of Almighty God are omnipotence and omnipresence. In other words, though there was no human being present to witness the event, Almighty God was. So I am declaring with all pure conscience that Almighty God of Heaven and Earth, bear me witness that what I am about to testify to is no fabrication but the truth and nothing but the truth.

Having said this by way of introduction, I shall go ahead and narrate further details concerning my supernatural experience.

Before I do so, I shall give a brief account of the circumstances leading to the mysterious happening, the manifestation that without doubt can aptly be described as being beyond what is natural

In previous chapters, I gave an account of my conversion, my desire to earn a profession before proceeding into ministry and how the Lord led me to medical school and provided for me throughout the time I was a student.

On graduation from medical school, I faced two options: (1) return to Ghana immediately to try and realise my plans. With little or no capital, I would have had to work in the public health system and adapt myself to it. What I have not mentioned is that I did consider returning to my home country to work in the public system. However, it became apparent to me that, like other doctors, I would be forced by the harsh economic conditions—in some cases, even if not directly—to demand money from patients before seeing them. That was the economic reality on the battlefield. That was never my dream, my vision. Indeed, my vision had all along been to provide healthcare affordable to all, and in such a way that no one should be denied healthcare by dint of affordability.

So, as my second option (2) I decided to set up a practice in Germany and, by that means, generate the funds. I would focus on my medical specialisation, save money and look out for partners to help me realise my goal.

Right from the outset I realised that working as a full-time doctor in a hospital would not permit me the flexibility needed for the realisation of my goal. I therefore pursued my specialisation as a family doctor or general practitioner (GP), which would enable me to work outside the hospital. Eventually, I set up my own one-man practice. One could compare me to a self-employed businessman.

Apart from the earnings from my GP work, I looked out for other sources of income to help realise my goal of building a charity clinic in Ghana. In the end I resorted to my gift of writing. I do not want to blow my trumpet before the whole world, but the fact remains that I am gifted with writing and have been writing on various themes and issues ever since my teenage days.

Some may consider my attitude and expectations as overoptimistic. Still, I dreamt of coming up with a best-seller that would rake in hundreds of thousands, if not millions, of Euros to support my charity hospital. Being my own boss in my practice, I could divide my time to suit that purpose.

The first book I published was *The Call that Changed My Life*. It is, in a nutshell, an account of how I made the journey all the way from my small village, Mpintimpi, to medical school in Germany. It would be followed by several other books on Christianity, health education, my experience of growing up in my small village Mpintimpi, etc.

Instead of the *millions* I had hoped for from my books to further my charitable goals in Ghana, the book business turned out instead to be a drain on my doctor's income, indeed haemorrhaging my doctor's income.

I shall provide a short explanation here. I was a self-publisher. I had to bear all the publishing costs upfront— editorial, proofreading, cover design, printing costs, PR & marketing, etc. I also purchased upfront a good number of copies for further sale –sometimes I was not able to sell all the stock leading to losses.

Mainly as a result of the losses from my publishing activities, I got into financial difficulty. Indeed, by the end of 2004 I stood on the brink of bankruptcy, defaulting not only on my mortgage payments for our home but also the rent of the practice.

It was at a time of deep financial crisis that one day I came across an advertisement in the leading German medical magazine, *Deutsches Ärzteblatt*, inviting German doctors to work in the UK.

Acting on the advert, I contacted the appropriate authorities for a licence to practice in the UK, which was granted. So I began to travel to the UK at the weekends to take on work in various parts of the country. I usually left Germany on a Friday and retuned either late on Sunday or early Monday morning. On average, I made two trips per month.

After about six months of traveling in such a manner to work in the UK, in February 2006 I moved with my family— Rita and our three children—to the UK. Working in the UK favoured me in several ways.

As a GP running my one-man practice in Germany, I had to do a good deal of bureaucracy on my own—which I did not have to do as a GP working for an agency. I submitted my availability to them at the beginning of every month and they assigned me jobs accordingly. At the end of each week, I submitted my time sheet and got paid based on the hours worked.

As a GP running my own practice, I had to pay the salary of my employees. (I had employed two full-time and two part-time workers.) Even when I was facing financial challenges, I had no other choice than to meet my contractual obligations to them. I was spared that headache as a locum GP in the UK working on my own.

In Germany I had to pay rent for the premises occupied by my practice, which was situated not far from the city centre. As might be expected of a property located in a prime location of a big European city, the rent could not be described as child's play.

My work as a doctor working for an agency on a part-time basis provided the flexibility I needed to combine my work as a doctor and author.

I booked just enough sessions to provide financial security for me and my family and I spent the available time writing my books.

In 2010, I wrote *Growing Up in a Small African Village*, in which I narrated the experience I had growing up in the deprived settings of my small village. It received good reviews from the Ghana Education Service. The Ghana Education Service recommended the book for use as a supplementary reader, giving head teachers a free hand to use their discretion to purchase the book for their schools.

Hoping to get regular orders from schools following the good review, I took a loan from my UK bank and printed a substantial number for further sale to secondary schools in my native country. Though I managed to sell a good proportion of the stock, for reasons I will spare the reader, the venture led to substantial losses.

Still desirous of earning money to build my charity hospital in Ghana, I invested in various ventures in the country, including tilapia farming on the Volta lake, a large artificial lake created for hydroelectric purposes. For various reasons, the details of which again I shall spare the reader, the ventures—instead of bringing profits—resulted in yet further substantial losses.

Meanwhile, not only was age telling against me, I was losing interest practising my trade in the UK. The UK and Europe at large could do without me as a doctor, I kept telling myself. What Europe needed from me, I also kept telling myself, was not my medical expertise, but rather my active engagement in spreading the Gospel of salvation—the good news of the Cross, the message of joy in the Lord, the message which alone can help lift the cloud of depression and hopelessness that has descended on the continent.

What a pity indeed—Europe that brought Christianity to Africa is now described as having evolved into a post-Christian community. And what has that led to? Hopelessness, spiritual misery, spiritual gloom. Rich in material wealth, Europe has become a spiritual desert.

Contributing towards a revival, an awakening was needed, indeed a fresh burst of the flame of the Holy Ghost, the flame that will rekindle the flame of the Gospel in Europe: that was what Europe needed from me and all others holding on to the Precious Treasure they have all but abandoned.

Then came the year 2020. In February, the coronavirus outbreak, which initially seemed to be a problem of far-away China, reached the shores of Europe. All of a sudden healthcare workers like myself were being described as frontline fighters in the war against the invisible enemy!

It is common knowledge that, apart from rare instances when individuals are forcefully recruited into the army and eventually end up on the war front against their will, the overwhelming majority of soldiers sent to the frontline in a conventional war signed up voluntarily for the army. They might have joined the army in peacetime with the threat of war a far distance from their minds. Yet when, contrary to their expectations, war breaks out and they are sent to defend their nations, they have no grounds to complain of being sent into harm's way.

And myself? Did I sign up to the healthcare profession to deal with such an aggressive and virulent virus? This has nothing to do with scaremongering. Yet based on what I have read from well-respected medical journals and sources concerning the ability of the virus not only to cause harm to the lungs, but also cause blood clots, strokes, kidney failure, etc., it has led me to conclude that unless humanity is able to come up with a cure and/or a vaccine any time soon, then we are in for real trouble.

Some may consider me a coward, or traitor, but based on the aforesaid, together with reports, initially from China, and later elsewhere that spoke of a good number of healthcare workers succumbing to the virus, I have reason to seriously consider quitting the profession at the earliest opportunity.

Still dependent on the income, I felt I needed to hang on for a while though. Every day I left home for work with a feeling of unease, that the invisible enemy, like a hungry lion, could pounce on me at any moment. Aware that, when push came to shove, when the time came when the invisible enemy appeared to be gaining the upper hand against me, I could call for Divine intervention, I was not overly scared.

Then came Saturday March 28. On waking up, I began to experience flu-like symptoms. Soon it dawned on me that I was dealing with something very different from a common flu. The bitter taste in the mouth, the loss of appetite, the muscle aches, the cough, the fever that persisted despite taking the maximum daily dosage of paracetamol, led me to believe that I had become a victim of this virulent microbe. Though the UK government stopped community testing on March 12, making it almost impossible for me to confirm my suspicion by way of a test, the unusual symptoms left no doubt in my mind I was dealing with a case of COVID-19.

At that stage, I decided to limit my counterattack not only to conventional medicine but also consult Doctor Jesus, the Doctor who knows no bounds.

Though I had until then been going through my usual daily prayer and meditation sessions, I decided to escalate things to seek help from a higher level.

Over the next several days I woke up in the night and, in prayer sessions lasting about an hour, spiritually wrestled with the microscopic organisms that had had the audacity to attempt for their own ends to hijack my body, in particular my precious lungs. What for heaven's sake were they doing in my body? On my knees and with my gaze towards heaven, I commanded them in Jesus' name to depart unconditionally from my body—and return no more!

My cries to Heaven did not go unheard. Indeed, on waking up in the morning, my temperature, though still raised, was the lowest I had measured since I was subjected to that unprovoked attack by the insubordinate microbes. Corona appears to be a die-hard foe, I tell you. Though defeated, their effect on my body in the form of raised temperature, muscle aches and the feeling of being generally unwell persisted for a few more days. Finally, just about two weeks after it all began, I felt strong enough to return to work.

A lot of good things are being said about the healthcare professionals fighting on the frontline. After that personal encounter with the spiteful and pernicious germ, however, I resolved to seek an exit from active duty at the very earliest opportunity.

Easier said than done! Indeed, much as I felt, out of abundance of caution, the need to leave the medical profession and go into full-time ministry, to exchange the stethoscope for the Bible, the reality on the ground made things not as straightforward as I would have wished. Not only did I need a regular income from my doctor's job to support myself and my family. I was also deep in debt from my Ghana investment that needed to be cleared.

It was in the midst of the confusion, the uncertainty, the frustration, the concern not only in regard to my health but also that of my family as a result of my "frontline duties on the battlefield" that I decided to embark on a three-day period of fasting starting from Thursday April 23, 2020, to seek the face of the Lord, to seek His direction for the uncertain future.

As I usually do when I fast and pray, I forgo food and fluids from getting up in the morning until just after 6 p.m. each day.

I don't know what the reader makes of fasting. Personally, throughout my over 40 years' walk with the Lord, I have engaged on this spiritual exercise on quite a regular basis.

In the early days following my conversion I was fasting for at least a day in every week. Of late, due to my busy schedule, I manage around once every fortnight.

My personal opinion is that God does not need the fasting of His children. It is His children rather who need the fasting to attain the state of mind that helps them draw close to Him in their prayers. Fasting, if you like, helps to dissipate the clouds of doubts within us, whilst strengthening our faith, faith that acts as a channel for the transmission of our prayer waves to Heaven.

Apart from prayer and meditating on God's words, the goal of the fasting had been to create the right atmosphere, the right spiritual mind to help me write sermons and mediations and reflect on some of the burning issues of our day from a Christian perspective.

Since October 2018, I have been publishing daily mediations on my Facebook page, THIS IS THE DAY, which has in the meantime attracted over half a million followers.

I made good progress in what I had set out to do on the first two days, writing a good number of sermons, meditations and short essays on various socio-political themes.

I woke up early on the third day Saturday, April 25, 2020.

After the usual morning prayer and meditation session, I was seated in front of my computer at 7:15. Apart from writing the sermons and meditations, I intended writing reflections on some of the social political themes of the day, from the Christian perspective. The world was gripped by the COVID-19 pandemic; there was no shortage of issues to reflect or comment on.

I turned on my laptop, opened a Word document and began my writings. To begin with I wrote a short reflection concerning the fact that, despite the breath-taking advances humanity had made over the last several years in the various fields of human endeavour—medicine, science, technology, space exploration, etc.—we had up till then not managed to find an antidote for the ghastly disease caused by a microbe that is said to measure approximately 50–200 nanometres (nm) in diameter. To put this into perspective, one nm is one-**billionth of a metre!**

I opened a new document and began reflecting on the lot of the poor and the deprived of the world in the midst of the coronavirus pandemic.

The poor were being called upon to stay at home as part of the lockdown of their countries. They were also being asked to observe social distancing. Having grown up in deprived conditions myself, and with the conditions existing in slums the likes of Agbogbloshie in Accra before my eyes, I just asked myself how such poor individuals who live from hand to mouth in such overcrowded settings were coping with the new reality.

At that moment, I recalled the words that are attributed to a poor man living in a shanty settlement in India: "Hunger will kill us before coronavirus!"

After saving the second document, I opened yet another new document and began to consider what to write next.

As I waited, thoughts concerning the way forward in my life began to fill my mind. I had planned starting a ministry, which I have christened the "Heaven and Earth Ministry", at the beginning of the year. The "Heaven" aspect would be dedicated to spreading the Gospel. The "Earth" aspect on its part would be devoted to helping solve some of the problems of the world, especially in the area of poverty alleviation.

Initially it would be internet-based, resorting to YouTube, Facebook, podcasting and other forms of modern communication. I had in the meantime set up a modest recording studio. The problem so far has been consistency, the need to upload regular material onto my various social media platforms so as to keep my audience engaged and, in so doing, help increase my following. My inability to do so boiled down to time. I needed to invest a good deal of time in the ministry to ensure growth—which I did not have, due mainly to the need for me to work as a doctor to support myself and the family.

Just then, I turned my attention to my laptop, still undecided as to what to write next.

I am sure many of my readers are familiar with Microsoft Word. On opening a new document, the words **Document— Word**, appear in the middle of the top of the page. As I stared at the blank page, all of a sudden, and from nowhere, the words *Wishes can never fill a sack* appeared on the top of the screen to replace the word **Document.** In other words, instead of **Document—Word,** the words **Wishes can never fill a sack— Word**, occupied the top of the page!

I stared at the screen, flabbergasted! *Wishes can never fill a sack*! How did that get there? I didn't write it; indeed, I didn't! I had until then never even come across the saying.

Wishes can never fill a sack! I guessed it meant something like—"One cannot achieve anything merely by wishing that something happen; one has instead to take concrete action towards the realisation of a set goal!" I consulted Google to make sure I had got it right—which happened to be the case.

Wishes cannot fill a sack! It is a clarion call to me to get up and take action! The Lord was in effect urging me to follow my wishes with concrete action. Instead of nesting myself in my comfort zone, in my job as a doctor that assured me an income from a job that no longer gave me job satisfaction, I should go ahead and act on my dreams and go into full-time ministry.

Wishes cannot fill a sack!
How can I receive such a message from the Good Shepherd and fail to act upon it? At a time when the world is going through such distressing moments, when the grim reality of death and suffering brought about by the coronavirus is everywhere evident, it is indeed important to remind the world

of the active involvement of the Ancient of Days in the affairs of the world.

For sure, I feel duty bound to do all I can to spread the message to the rest of the world. Of course, I am aware not everyone will believe my testimony; indeed, that others may even deride me, look upon me with scorn—yet I won't be perturbed since I know I am bearing testimony to the truth.

As a direct consequence of the mysterious encounter, I have decided to bid farewell to active medical practice and dedicate myself fully to spreading the Word of God. I have given myself a transitional period of a maximum of 12 months to bring about the change.

Wishes can never fill a sack!

Though the message was directed at me, the Lord may be speaking to you as well, dear reader.

I am not implying this message is applicable to any selfish wish you are harbouring in your heart. Maybe you're a young man looking for a partner; your heart may be reaching out for a young lady in the congregation. Even though she, by her actions, has indicated she is not interested in you, you are still determined to persevere. Well, this message would not apply under such circumstances.

The reverse is of course also true—a young lady pursuing a gentleman who is not interested in her cannot lay claim to the message and pursue him still.

Yet another example—you may be entertaining the thought of becoming a millionaire. The Lord indeed may want to bless you abundantly, even make a multi-millionaire out of you. No cross, no crown. Following that saying, He may want to train you first, put you through a series of life lessons, equip you to be in a position to handle the abundant wealth you will be exposed to. Until that happens, any stepping out on your own in the quest for the millions would be presumptuous, could even lead to disaster.

On the other hand, if you have prayed to the Lord to guide you in setting up a charity to provide for the poor, go out to spread His word either in your country or in a foreign land. Indeed if you have prayed to the Lord for wisdom in embarking in ventures that will further His Kingdom, and if, after having prayed over such a venture, you feel deep in your spirit that you have His permission, if you are still dithering, procrastinating, nesting in your comfort zone, not bold enough to venture into the unknown—the Lord's message to you is *Wishes can never fill a sack!*

The Lord is urging you to summon up courage and step out of your comfort zone. Even if it implies stepping out into deep darkness, be assured that since it is the Loving Father who is sending you out, He will also provide for you. He is not known to abandon His own, or leave His precious ones in the dark. Rest assured, He will send the needed rays of light to guide you through the darkness, to a safe and sure destination.

Wishes can never fill a sack!
I believe the message is meant for the church as a whole. It is generally felt that the church needs revival in a world that has generally turned atheistic. In Europe, for example, the talk these days is of the continent having evolved into a post-Christian society.

If the church is sensing the need for revival, we should not only harbour that wish. The Holy Spirit is instead urging us to take concrete steps towards the realisation of the objective.

Instead of barricading ourselves in the comforts of our church buildings for Sunday worship that has become repetitive and devoid of "the Holy Ghost fire", instead of limiting our activities to the comforts of our church buildings, we could, for example, embark on street evangelisation; visit prisons to speak the word of hope to the hopeless; visit hospitals to speak a word of cheer to the sick and down-hearted.

For sure, it is not enough for a church located in a deprived area to pray only for the well-being of the poor, the impoverished, the sick in the neighbourhood; the congregation is also being urged to take concrete steps to alleviate the suffering—for example by setting up a food bank, a second-hand clothing outlet to hand out free clothes to the penniless, a clinic to provide affordable health care, etc.

Wishes can never fill a sack! It is, indeed, high time God's people ventured out into the world to make a difference, to make their light shine!

Epilogue

Battered from all sides but not uprooted

S omeone reading through the testimonies recounted in this
book could be inclined to conclude that my Christian walk
has been relatively smooth, that I have always received a quick
answer to my prayers whenever I found myself in trouble.

As the testimonies I have delivered in this book bear
witness, the Lord has on several occasion stepped into my life
to deliver me from trouble and danger and also to provide for
my needs.

That does not mean, though, that I have been spared
suffering, predicaments, woes, etc. or that I have always
received prompt answers to my prayers. That has not been my
experience. Indeed how do I expect to be exempt from
suffering, woes, trials, tribulations, etc., when the giants of the
Faith, the likes of Peter, Paul, Stephen, etc., were not spared
the rod (as it were); indeed, did not have all their prayers
answered—at least not in the way they might have wished.

> *Three times I pleaded with the Lord to take it away
> from me. But he said to me, "My grace is sufficient for
> you, for my power is made perfect in weakness."
> Therefore I will boast all the more gladly about my
> weaknesses, so that Christ's power may rest on me.
> That is why, for Christ's sake, I delight in weaknesses,
> in insults, in hardships, in persecutions, in difficulties.
> For when I am weak, then I am strong.*
>
> 2 Corinthians 12:8–10

I have not always been spared trouble, my dear reader. Some of the problems have persisted, despite my persistent plea to heaven to take them away.

I am working on a book dedicated to the trials, obstacles and challenges I have encountered in my Christian walk.

I feel duty-bound to do exactly that; in particular, for the sake of the young convert to the faith. Indeed, for the sake of the new convert in the faith, it is imperative on my part to paint a balanced picture of my Christian experience, to make them aware that trials, afflictions, persecutions, etc., could be part and parcel of the Christian journey.

As just mentioned, I am working on a book dedicated to my trials. For the sake of those who may not come across it, I shall touch briefly on a few.

The most emotionally tormenting and spiritually challenging cross I have borne over the years, and continue to bear even as I am writing this account, involves my son David, the second of our three children, who is plagued with the condition of autism. He is not only incontinent for stool and urine; his behaviour is also very challenging, to say the least. His hyperactive behaviour leads him, among other things, frequently to hop and jump around the home, in the process— unintentionally I must stress—causing damage to furniture, glass, mobile phones, wallpaper, CD players, etc. I have lost count of the number of times we have had to replace damaged furniture and gadgets, as well as pay for the repair of damaged walls, windows, heating radiators, etc.

As expected, we have over the years not ceased from praying for Divine intervention. We have not limited our prayer efforts to ourselves, for we have also taken him to numerous prayer and healing events—by well-known as well as lesser known men and women of God.

Someone will be inclined to put the question to me—if your God is so good, why has He not intervened to heal David?

My reaction to that may be summed up as follows:

How dare you, my good friend, put that question to me? Do you expect me, a mere human being, to be in a position to read the mind of Almighty God? I can only refer you to a passage of scripture as recorded in John 9: 1–3 (KJV):

As he went along, he saw a man blind from birth. His disciples asked him, "Rabbi, who sinned, this man or his parents, that he was born blind?"

"Neither this man nor his parents sinned," said Jesus, "but this happened so that the works of God might be displayed in him."

The Enemy has various ways of testing the resolve of God's children, challenging the faith of servants of the Living Jesus.

Earlier in my narration, I touched on my childhood dream of setting up a charity hospital. As a way of raising money for the venture I engaged in various business ventures in my native Ghana. Ouch! How often did the venture become a victim of deception, fraud, dishonesty from various suppliers, business associates, customers, etc.

As if that were not enough, one afternoon I got a call from Ghana to inform me that the makeshift structure put up to serve as a warehouse for the books I was supplying to the Ghana Education Service was on fire. In the end, the whole structure was burnt to ashes and, with it, the thousands of books kept there.

You thought that was the only harm caused by the fire? Misfortunes never come singly, so the saying goes. The blazing fire might have had that in mind, for it decided to take a leap into the company delivery van parked a few metres from the building. In the end the front side of the vehicle, including the engine compartment, was burnt beyond repair.

I have selected only two items from the catalogue of woes that have visited me over the last few years. I have experienced not a few tumultuous times in my Christian walk, especially in regard to my finances.

As I experienced one setback after another, it came to a point when I exclaimed in exasperation: "Hey, Master Jesus, what is going on here? Why are you not preserving me from these series of trials and misfortunes!" There were indeed times when I was inclined to repeat the words of Gideon as found in Judges 6: 13 (KJV):

And Gideon said unto him, Oh my Lord, if the LORD be with us, why then is all this befallen us? and where be all his miracles which our fathers told us of, saying, Did not the LORD bring us up from Egypt? but now the LORD hath forsaken us, and delivered us into the hands of the Midianites.

In my moments of despair, the Lord's promise to His children delivered through the Apostle Paul in 1 Corinthians 10:13 provided me solace:

*There hath no temptation taken you but such as is common to man: but God **is** faithful, who will not suffer you to be tempted above that ye are able; but will with the temptation also make a way to escape, that ye may be able to bear it.*

Instead of adopting a defeatist attitude, seeing only a half empty bottle, I encouraged and motivated myself, even resolved to keep silent and wait on the good time of the Great Comforter.

Then came the morning of April 25, 2020 and, out of the blue, the Rock of Ages manifested Himself in a way and manner beyond my imagination:

The Lord is alive; yes indeed, He is alive forevermore.

May His Name be blessed and glorified!

www.ingramcontent.com/pod-product-compliance
Lightning Source LLC
Chambersburg PA
CBHW071623040426

42452CB00009B/1465